STICKER ENCYCLOPEDIA

AROUND THE WORLD

T0179958

DK | Penguin Random House

US editor Liz Searcy
US senior editor Shannon Beatty
Senior editors James Mitchem, Roohi Sehgal
Project editor Kritika Gupta
Senior art editor Rachael Parfitt
Project art editors Kanika Kalra, Roohi Rais
Assistant art editors Bhagyashree Nayak, Simran Lakhiani
DTP designers Dheeraj Singh, Rohit Rojal
Project picture researcher Sakshi Saluja
Jacket coordinator Issy Walsh
Jacket designer Rashika Kachroo
Managing editors Penny Smith, Monica Saigal
Managing art editor Mabel Chan
Deputy managing art editor Ivy Sengupta
Assistant producer, preproduction Abi Maxwell
Senior producer Amy Knight
Delhi team head Malavika Talukder
Publishing manager Francesca Young
Creative directors Helen Senior, Clare Baggaley
Publishing director Sarah Larter

First American Edition, 2020
Published in the United States by DK Publishing
1450 Broadway, Suite 801, New York, New York 10018

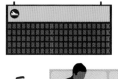

A catalog record for this book is available from the Library of Congress.
ISBN 978-1-4654-9432-0

DK books are available at special discounts when purchased in bulk for
sales promotions, premiums, fund-raising, or educational use.

For details, contact:
DK Publishing Special Markets, 1450 Broadway, Suite 801,
New York, New York 10018
SpecialSales@dk.com

Printed and bound in China

A WORLD OF IDEAS:
SEE ALL THERE IS TO KNOW

www.dk.com

Contents

Where to go?	4–5
Popular travel sights	6–7
At the airport	8–9
On the runway	10–11
Types of aircraft	12–13
To the gate	14–15
Europe	16–17
More of Europe	18–19
North America	20–21
More of North America	22–23
South America	24–25
More of South America	26–27
Asia	28–29
More of Asia	30–31
Africa	32–33
More of Africa	34–35
Australia	36–37
More of Australia	38–39
Vacation journal	40
Sticker fun!	42–71

Picture credits:

The publisher would like to thank the following for their kind permission to reproduce their photographs:
(Key: a-above; b-below/bottom; c-center; f-far; l-left; r-right; t-top)

1 123RF.com: elvetica (cla); Roberto Scandola (tr). **Dorling Kindersley:** Musee du Louvre, Paris (clb). **Dreamstime.com:** Dima1970 (ftr); Javarman (cra); Nataliia Velishchuk (crb). **iStockphoto.com:** sag29 (cla/Jordan). **2 Dreamstime.com:** Elenatur (bl); Macrovector (tr). **iStockphoto.com:** Frankhildebrand (ttl). **3 Alamy Stock Photo:** D. Hurst (tr). **Dreamstime.com:** Yevgenii Movliev (tr). **6 123RF.com:** Roberto Scandola (c). **Dreamstime.com:** Maxsaf (cr). **iStockphoto.com:** Oksana_Gracheva (tr); sag29 (cl). **7 Alamy Stock Photo:** Nature Picture Library (cl). **Dreamstime.com:** Niradj (cra); Rimma Z (ca, ca / Dragon). **iStockphoto.com:** agustavop (tl); pniesen (crb). **8 Alamy Stock Photo:** EuroStyle Graphics (crb). **9 123RF.com:** elvetica (bl). **10 Dreamstime.com:** Ccat82 (bl). **12 Dreamstime.com:** Icefront (cr). **15 Dreamstime.com:** Andrey Dybrovskiy (br). **16 123RF.com:** olgatik (b). **17 123RF.com:** rawpixel (cra, ca, ca / tags, fcl); Takashi Honma (tr); Kheira Benkada (cla). **Dorling Kindersley:** Musee du Louvre, Paris (ca / Mona Lisa). **18 Alamy Stock Photo:** IanDagnall Computing (ca). **Dreamstime.com:** Artinspiring (cra); Ccat82 (bla). **19 Alamy Stock Photo:** Gary E Perkin (br). **Getty Images:** Matthew Lloyd (cl). **21 123RF.com:** captainvector (b). **Dreamstime.com:** Raymond Kasprzak / Rkasprzak (ca). **22 Depositphotos Inc:** Alhovik (cra); Olia_Nikolina (fcra). **Dreamstime.com:** Ccat82 (bl / Background); Viktoriia Protsak (tr). **22–23 Dreamstime.com:** Ihor Smishko (Background). **23 Alamy Stock Photo:** ZUMA Press, Inc. (cb). **Dreamstime.com:** Kontur-vid (bc). **iStockphoto.com:** Holcy (cr). **25 123RF.com:** Stanislav Kozhukov (c/People). **Dreamstime.com:** Izabela 23 (tc); Dima1970 (c); Dreamzdesigner (cb). **26 Getty Images:** Kelly Cheng (cra); Vanina Montano / EyeEm (crb). **iStockphoto.com:** Alfribeiro (clb). **27 iStockphoto.com:** David Bautista (cl); Buenaventuramariano (tl); Patrick_Gijsbers (cra). **28 Dreamstime.com:** Elenatur (cra). **29 Dreamstime.com:** Burlesck (br); Srlee2 (bl). **30 123RF.com:** elvetica (b). **Dreamstime.com:** Ccat82 (tr / Background); Vvoevale (vlb). **iStockphoto.com:** prabhjits (fclb). **31 Dreamstime.com:** Ccat82 (b / Background); Macrovector (tr); Kanjanee Chaisin (cr); Vector Moon (bc). **33 123RF.com:** Mykola Nisolovskyi (cla). **34–35 Dreamstime.com:** Goldghost (Background); Derplan Xiii (b). **35 Alamy Stock Photo:** Chronicle (cb). **Dreamstime.com:** Ccat82 (t / Background); Andrey Gudkov (b). **36 123RF.com:** elenabsl; Stanislav Kozhukov (People under umbrella); Anna Zakharchenko (Icons). **37 Dreamstime.com:** Ccat82 (t / Background). **38 Dreamstime.com:** Ernest Akayeu (clb); Nataliia Velishchuk (cra); Julian Peters (bl); Yevgenii Movliev (b). **Getty Images:** Jeff Hunter (cr). **iStockphoto.com:** Blulz60 (crb); Bicho_raro (cl). **39 Dreamstime.com:** ActiveLines (Background); Godruma (cr). **42 123RF.com:** elvetica (bc); Roberto Scandola (cb). **Dreamstime.com:** Maksym Kapliuk (tr). **iStockphoto.com:** Oksana_Gracheva (crb); sag29 (bl). **43 123RF.com:** Roberto Scandola (ca). **Dreamstime.com:** pniesen (tr/Great Wall China), cr); Iuliia Bereznikova (c). **iStockphoto.com:** pniesen (tr). **46 Dorling Kindersley:** The Real Aeroplane Company (clb). **47 Alamy Stock Photo:** Viktoriia Khyzhniak (cla). **48 123RF.com:** Ed Brown (c); D. Hurst (tc, cla, cb); Invictus SARL (c). **Dreamstime.com:** Pavel Chagochkin (clb). **iStockphoto.com:** Jondpatton (bc). **50 123RF.com:** Krisztian Miklosy (tl, cb); olgatik (c). **Dreamstime.com:** Javarman (cra); Reidlphoto (br). **Getty Images:** Joe Daniel Price (tc, cb/The Shard). **iStockphoto.com:** TomasSereda (tc/Sagrada Familia, bc). **51 123RF.com:** Evgenii Naumov (cb/Muffin). **Alamy Stock Photo:** Lifestyle pictures (tl); World History Archive (tc); Zsolt Repasy (c); Gary E Perkin (cb/French Water Jousters). **Dreamstime.com:** Artinspiring (c); Roberto Giovannini (r/Flags). **Getty Images:** Pablo Blazquez Dominguez (cl). **iStockphoto.com:** Dr_Chinarro (tc/Van Gogh).

54–55 Depositphotos Inc: wikki33 (bc). **54 123RF.com:** Bohdana Bergmannova (crb); captainvector (cl); Diana Johanna Velasquez (fcra). **Dreamstime.com:** Olga Bogatyrenko (tc/Capitol building); Minyun Zhou / Minyun9260 (ttl); Jeremyreds (tc); Chase Dekker / Chasedekker (ca); Homoerectuss (cra); Nenilkime (fcrb); Dima1970 (bl). **55 123RF.com:** Anna Zakharchenko (c). **Alamy Stock Photo:** Ian Dagnall (clb); Bert Hoferichter (c/Georgian Bay); RM USA (cr/Bowling Ball Beach); ZUMA Press, Inc. (br). **Dorling Kindersley:** Linda Pitkin (fclb). **Dreamstime.com:** Vasile Bobirnac (fcra); Brian Kushner (tc); Maksym Kapliuk (tr); Vladimir Sviracevic (ftr); Ibrandify (cra); Ylivdesign (cr); Valeriy Kaplun (fcr). **Getty Images:** Pchoui (ftl); rusm (cl). **iStockphoto.com:** Frankhildebrand (ca). **58 123RF.com:** Morley Read/atelopus (br); Natthapon Ngamnithiporn (cl/Shirt). **Dreamstime.com:** Chernetskaya (tl, tc, cb/Backpacks and sunglasses); Dechev (tc/Bottle, clb); Pixattitude (tr); Volodymyrkrasyuk (cla, cb/Yoga mat); Irina Kryvasheina (ca, cb); Dmitriyrnd (cra); Liliia Khuzhakhmetova (cla/Sport equipment, c/Phone, c/Sunglasses); Olga Popova (c); Kewuwu (fcl); Venusangel (cl); Macbibi (crb); Renato Machado (crb/Rio De Janeiro). **59 123RF.com:** Evgenii Naumov (c/Amusement Park); nito500 (cb). **Dreamstime.com:** Izabela 23 (c); Ccat82 (cl/Background). **Getty Images:** Kelly Cheng (ca); Vanina Montano/EyeEm (fcra). **iStockphoto.com:** Alfribeiro (cra); David Bautista (ca/Orchids); Patrick_Gijsbers (cra/Chimborazo Volcano); Buenaventuramariano (fcra/Andean Condor). **62 123RF.com:** Aprilvalery (cb/Food and Drinks); Songquan Deng (cra); Sarawuth Wantha (cra/Chocolate Hills); elvetica (c/Banana); Anna Zakharchenko (c/Crab); Evgenii Naumov (clb/Burger, br/Pear). **Dreamstime.com:** Elenatur (br); Srlee2 (tl); Iuliia Kuzenkova (ftr); Andrii Vergeles (fcra); Somchai Somsanitangkul / Tank_isara (cra). **iStockphoto.com:** MikeFuchslocher (tr). **63 123RF.com:** Aprilvalery (c, cb/Tomato); Pylyp Sereda / Iappenno (ca); Noppakun Wiropart (ttl); tonarinokeroro (cla); elvetica (bl); Evgenii Naumov (fbl, cb). **Alamy Stock Photo:** Natasha McGoram (ca/Kuang Si Falls). **Depositphotos Inc:** tatisol (tc). **Dreamstime.com:** Burlesck (ftr). **66 123RF.com:** Mykola Nisolovskyi (cb, crb, cr/Africa, cra/Jeep); Diana Johanna Velasquez (tc). **Dreamstime.com:** Atosan (c/Delta); Sergii Kolesnyk (tl, cra); Paul Vinten (tc, bc); Volodymyr Byrdyak (c, cr); Kseniia Zagrebaeva (cl, br). **iStockphoto.com:** Guenterguni (cla, bl). **66–67 123RF.com:** Diana Johanna Velasquez (tc). **67 123RF.com:** Macrovector (ca, cb); Mykola Nisolovskyi (b). **Alamy Stock Photo:** Watchtheworld (c). **Dreamstime.com:** Andrey Gudkov (tc); Dzianis Martynenka (c); Evgenii Khadeev (cra). **70–71 123RF.com:** Anna Zakharchenko (Icons/ beach, Icons). **70 123RF.com:** Stanislav Kozhukov (b/People). **Alamy Stock Photo:** Dimple Patel (c). **Dreamstime.com:** Anaanorl (ca/Rock); Tanya Puntti (ca); Radoslav Cajkovic (ca/Sopoaga Waterfall); Mything (Background); Martin Valigursky (tr); Fedecandoniphoto (cra); VanderWolfImages (cr). **iStockphoto.com:** Smitt (fcr). **71 Dreamstime.com:** ActiveLines (br); Julian Peters (cl); Ernest Akayeu (ca); Dragoneye (bl); Nataliia Velishchuk (ca/Scuba diver). **Fotolia:** Eric Isselee (crb). **Getty Images:** Jeff Hunter (tc). **iStockphoto.com:** Bicho_raro (cla)

Cover images: Front: **123RF.com:** elvetica clb, Brian Kinney cla, Krisztian Miklosy cb, Mykola Nisolovskyi bl, Anna Zakharchenko cb/ (Camera); **Alamy Stock Photo:** D. Hurst tr; **Dreamstime.com:** Chase Dekker / Chasedekker cr, Sonya Etchison tl, Jeremyreds fclb, Sergii Kolesnyk br, Micha? Rojek / Michalrojek (Background), Reidlphoto crb; **Getty Images:** Pchoui c; Back: **Dreamstime.com:** Dragoneye bl, Lillia Khuzhakhmetova crb, Renato Machado cr, Micha? Rojek / Michalrojek (Background), VanderWolfImages cla; **iStockphoto.com:** Guenterguni tc, MikeFuchslocher tr, Bicho_raro cb

All other images © Dorling Kindersley
For further information see: www.dkimages.com.

Where to go?

Deciding where in the world to visit and what kind of trip you and your family might enjoy can be tricky. There are so many wonderful countries to visit and exciting things to do. So let's get planning for an amazing adventure!

Around the world

Read the hints and tips to help you guess the countries and place the sticker flags!

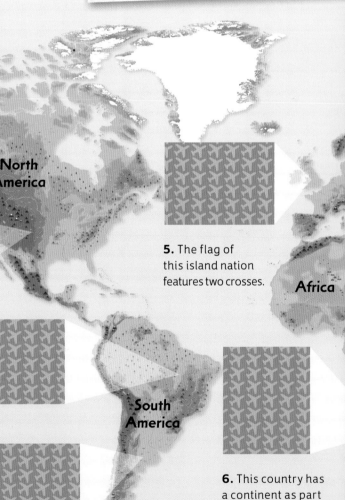

1. This country is the second largest in the world. Its flag has a maple leaf in the middle.

2. There are 50 states in this country. Its flag is made up of stars and stripes.

3. Famous for its soccer, this country has a flag featuring a blue globe with a starry sky.

4. This country is the second biggest in South America. It has a blue-and-white striped flag with a sun in the middle.

5. The flag of this island nation features two crosses.

6. This country has a continent as part of its name. Its flag is very colorful.

North America

South America

Africa

What kind of vacation?

Use this fun chart to help you decide what type of vacation you'd like to go on. Stick the stickers on your favorites!

Start

Do you want to go somewhere warm and sunny?

No

Yes

Q&A

Which country has the most colorful flag? Here's a clue: it's on this page!

Take turns thinking of a country or city that begins with each letter of the alphabet, for example, Argentina, Brussels, Canada, and so on. You're out if you can't think of a place. The winner is the last person still in.

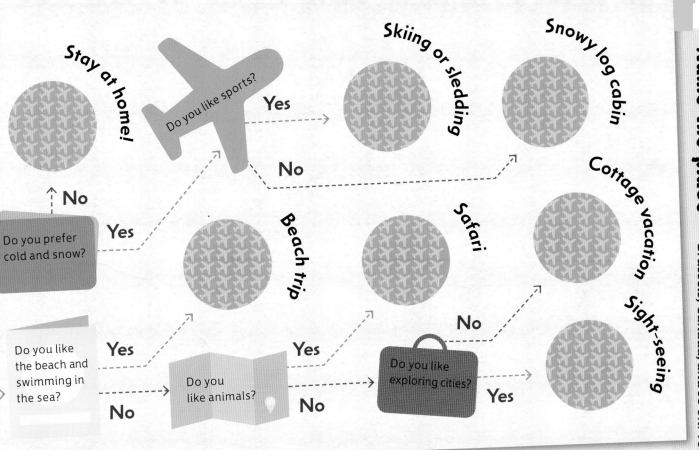

Stay at home!

Do you like sports?

Yes — Skiing or sledding — Snowy log cabin

No

Do you prefer cold and snow?

No

Yes

Beach trip

Safari

Cottage vacation

Sight-seeing

Do you like the beach and swimming in the sea?

Yes

No

Do you like animals?

Yes

No

Do you like exploring cities?

No

Yes

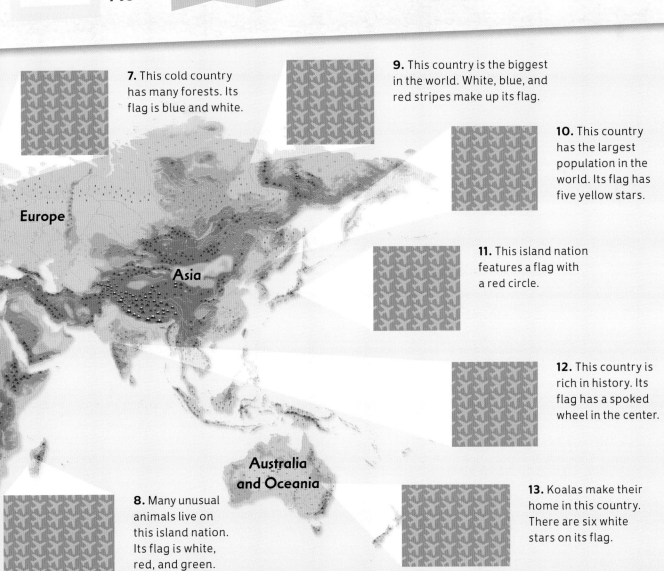

Europe

Asia

Australia and Oceania

7. This cold country has many forests. Its flag is blue and white.

8. Many unusual animals live on this island nation. Its flag is white, red, and green.

9. This country is the biggest in the world. White, blue, and red stripes make up its flag.

10. This country has the largest population in the world. Its flag has five yellow stars.

11. This island nation features a flag with a red circle.

12. This country is rich in history. Its flag has a spoked wheel in the center.

13. Koalas make their home in this country. There are six white stars on its flag.

5

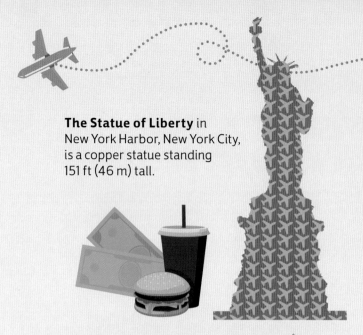

The Statue of Liberty in New York Harbor, New York City, is a copper statue standing 151 ft (46 m) tall.

Spectacular **northern lights** fill the night sky of Norway between September and March.

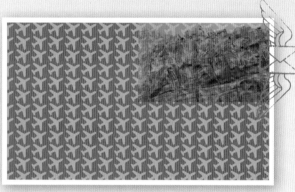

Petra is also called the "Rose City." It is famous for its hand-cut caves, temples, and tombs made from pink sandstone. It was built almost 2,000 years ago.

The **Iguazú Falls** are a group of waterfalls that look like a long horseshoe. It is the largest waterfall system in the world.

Popular travel sights

Q&A

Which Japanese city is called "the nation's kitchen?"

The world is full of places to visit. Some are close to the beach, others to the mountains. Some are old historical monuments, while others are modern skyscrapers. Here are some popular sights to visit on your travels.

Make your own travel bucket list of all the places you want to visit. Write down the names of the sights you would like to see. You can even use stickers to make your list look exciting.

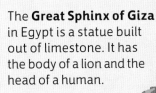

The **Great Sphinx of Giza** in Egypt is a statue built out of limestone. It has the body of a lion and the head of a human.

St. Basil's Cathedral in Moscow, Russia, has nine small churches. They are connected with galleries and passageways.

The **Great Wall of China** is 5,500 miles (8,850 km) long. It was built about 600 years ago.

Osaka in Japan is also called "the nation's kitchen." The Kuromon Ichiba Market is one of the most popular destinations in Osaka.

Hawa Mahal or "Palace of Winds" in Jaipur, India, is made from red and pink sandstone. It is a five-story building with 953 decorated windows.

Vaadhoo Island, in the Maldives, is most visited after dark. The tiny organisms in the water make it appear electric blue.

The **Colosseum** in Rome is the largest open theater in the world. As many as 50,000 people could be seated in it.

The **Great Barrier Reef** in Australia is the world's largest coral reef. It has more than 2,900 reefs.

Airport bingo

Write two lists of people or objects you might find at the airport (for example, a person with an orange bag). Give one list to a friend or family member, then race to see who can find all the things on their list first.

At the airport

Welcome to the airport! This busy, bustling place is the gateway to the rest of the world. Are you ready to hop on a plane and start your exciting trip? Grab your bags, passport, and ticket, then head to the check-in counter.

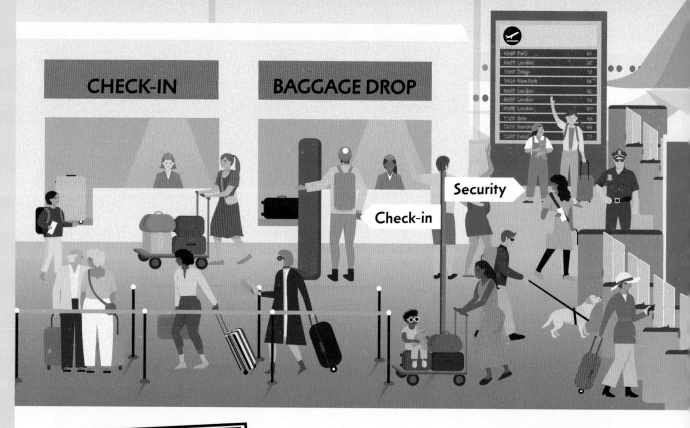

CHECK-IN

BAGGAGE DROP

Check-in

Security

Your ticket

Are you all ready to go? Fill in your plane ticket.

Plane ticket	Boarding pass
Name	Flight number
Airline	Departure time
Departure	Arrival time
Arrival	Seat number

How many?

This airport is super busy! Write down how many of these things you can find.

Teddy bears

Airline staff dressed in red

Security guards

Find and circle

1. Someone listening to music
2. A striped suitcase
3. Twins in a stroller
4. Someone with a guide dog
5. A child on a luggage cart

Check-in checklist

Find the missing stickers to make sure you have everything you need for check-in. Let's hope you haven't left anything at home!

Luggage

Passport

Tickets

Entertainment

Money

Are you checking any bags? Write down how much they weigh.

On the runway

The airport's runway is always busy! Planes come in to land, then take off again. Passengers get on board, and luggage is loaded into the cargo hold. All the workers have very important jobs to do.

Q&A

Which airport has the longest paved runway in the world?

Airport facts

There are about 1,200 airports across the world. Some of them are big enough to handle more than 18 million passengers every year.

1 Dubai International Airport, UAE
This is one of the busiest airports in the world. In 2018, this airport handled 89.1 million passengers.

2 College Park Airport in Maryland
The oldest operational airport in the world, College Park Airport was established by the Wright brothers in 1909.

3 Istanbul Airport, Turkey
The new airport in Istanbul is one of the largest and most modern airports in the world. It also employs a fleet of humanoid robots to assist passengers.

4 El Alto International Airport, Bolivia
Built at an altitude of 13,325 ft (4,061 m), El Alto International Airport is one of the highest airports in the world.

5 Qamdo Bamda Airport, China
The Qamdo Bamda Airport in China has the longest paved runway in the world at 18,045 ft (5,500 m).

Sticker fun

Here's a scene from the runway. Add stickers to show what you can see on it.

Airport shuttle

Luggage carrier

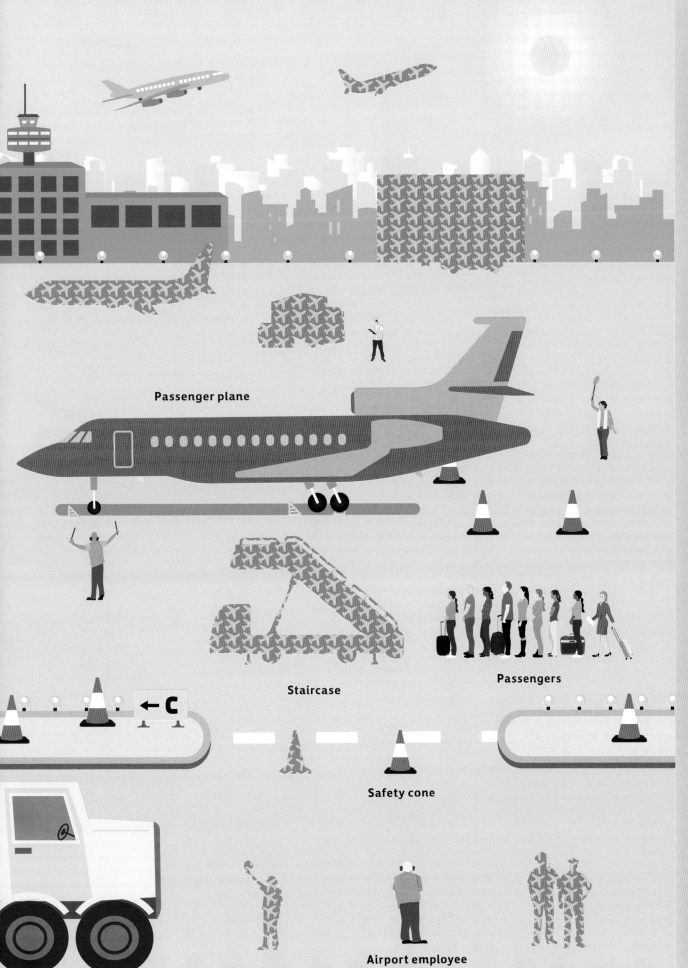

Passenger plane

Staircase

Passengers

Safety cone

Airport employee

Types of aircraft

Aircraft are vehicles that can fly. They help us make long-distance journeys in less time. There are many different types of aircraft. Here are some of them.

Helicopters

Helicopters, or choppers, use fast-spinning blades to fly through the air. The blades, or rotors, lift the helicopters and move them forward.

Biplanes

Biplanes were the most common aircraft in the early days of flight. They were called biplanes because they had two pairs of wings.

Passenger planes

Passenger planes are also called airliners. They carry people from one place to the other.

Balloon aircraft

Balloon aircraft are filled with gases like hydrogen or helium to help them stay afloat in the sky. These aircraft depend mostly on wind to steer them.

Supersonic planes

Supersonic planes can fly faster than the speed of sound, which is 750 mph (1,196 kph).

Gliders

Gliders are aircraft that have no engines. They are small and light.

Leisure aircraft

Leisure aircraft are small in size and are used mostly for training, private transportation, and recreational flying.

Jet planes

Jet planes can fly faster and higher than passenger planes. They are widely used as fighter planes because of their speed.

Seaplanes

Seaplanes are designed to land on water. They have waterproof hulls and floaters instead of wheels. Seaplanes can land on open stretches of water.

1. Which aircraft is also called an airliner?   2. Are there any planes that can land on the sea?   3. Name the aircraft that can fly without an engine.   4. Which plane can fly faster than the speed of sound?

13

To the gate

Q&A
What time do you have to be at the departure gate? Check your ticket to be sure.

Once your gate number appears on the departure board, it's almost time to get on the plane. Follow the signs to your gate, and get ready to board the airplane.

Find your way

The airport is so big and busy that it can feel like a maze. Give yourself plenty of time to make your way through the terminal. Can you find your gate?

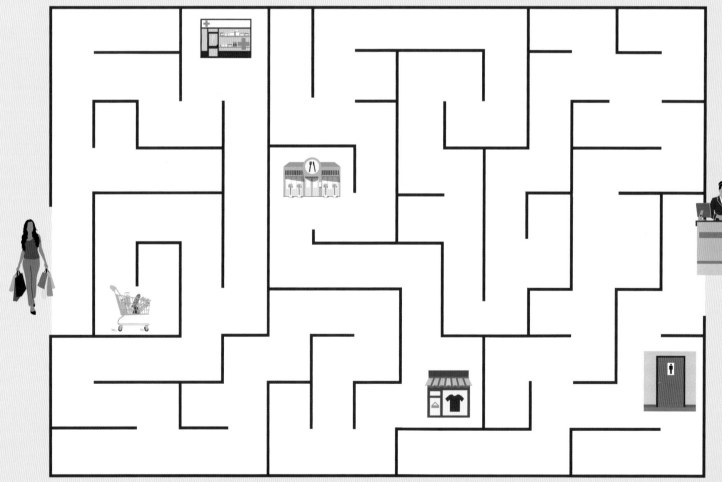

Follow the signs to find the way to your gate.

✈ DEPARTURES

ROME	08:00
SYDNEY	08:30
CAIRO	09:00
PARIS	10:30
SHANGHAI	12:00
NEW YORK	12:15

What time?

Don't be late for boarding! Match the departure times on the board with the clock stickers.

TRAVEL DATA

Singapore Changi Airport is so big that it has a pool on the roof, a movie theater, and even a butterfly garden.

Where on Earth?

The departure board has muddled up the letters. Can you unscramble the letters to find out the destination cities? Use the pictures to help you.

PAISR
NWE RYHO
CAOIR
SYEYND
REOM
SHAAHIGN

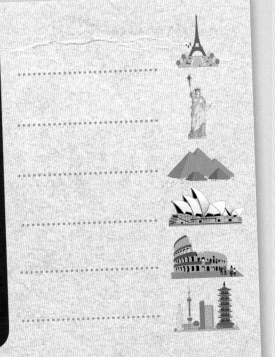

Europe

Although it's the second-smallest continent, Europe has a wide range of amazing places to see, such as mountains and forests or incredible buildings, such as the famous Eiffel Tower in Paris, France.

Europe

Eiffel Tower

DID YOU KNOW?

Gustave Eiffel, who designed the Eiffel Tower, also helped build the Statue of Liberty in New York.

Quickest line

It looks like everyone wants to visit the Eiffel Tower today! Can you figure out which line will be the quickest?

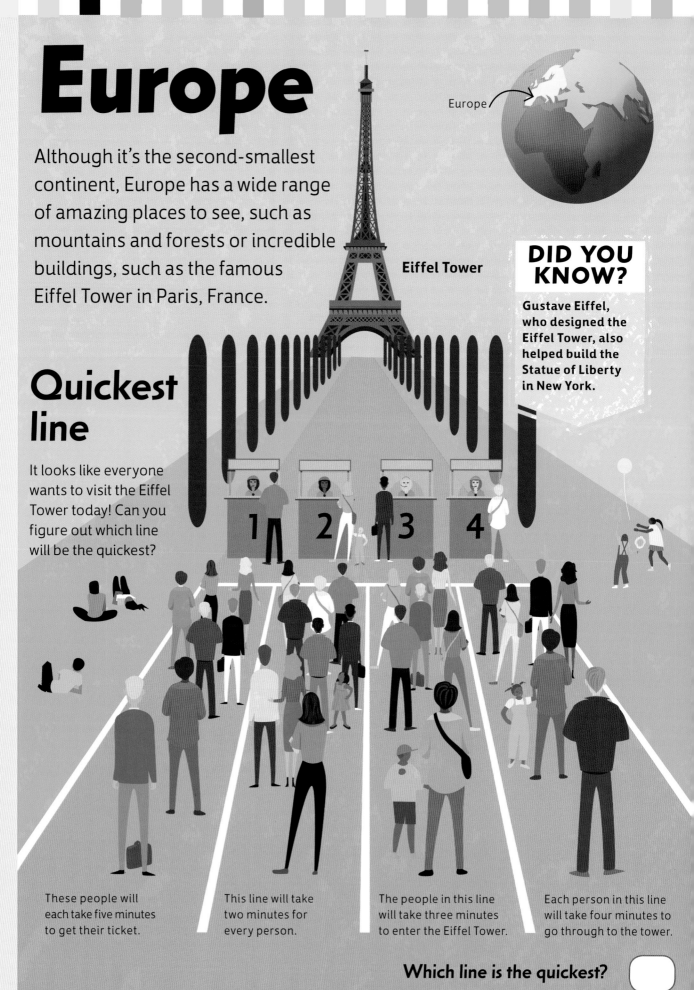

These people will each take five minutes to get their ticket.

This line will take two minutes for every person.

The people in this line will take three minutes to enter the Eiffel Tower.

Each person in this line will take four minutes to go through to the tower.

Which line is the quickest?

Souvenir shopping

No trip to Paris is complete without bringing back some souvenirs. If you have 14 euros (€) and would like to bring home two souvenirs, which ones could you afford?

€5

€11

€7

PARIS

€10

How much money would you have left?

Terrific towers

There are lots of amazing buildings in Europe, and some are super interesting! Add the correct sticker to each tower's name.

The tallest building in Britain looks just as its name suggests.

The Shard

Enjoy the view of the French capital from this tall tower.

Is this building in Italy going to fall over?

This interesting building in Belgium is made of six spheres connected by tubes.

Although this church in Barcelona isn't finished, it's still stunning!

Eiffel Tower

Leaning Tower of Pisa

Atomium

La Sagrada Familia

More of Europe

Europe is connected to Asia, and together they make up one big supercontinent called Eurasia. Russia and Turkey are counted as part of both Europe and Asia.

European artists

Europe is home to several famous artists who have added to the rich heritage of the continent.

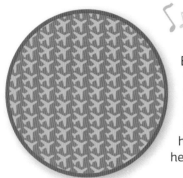

Born in Germany, **Ludwig van Beethoven** (1770–1827) is one of the most famous composers and pianists in history. He published his first composition when he was only 12 years old.

The Italian sculptor, painter, and architect **Michelangelo** (1475–1564) was considered one of the greatest artists of the Renaissance period.

Vincent van Gogh (1853–1890) was a Dutch painter. He is among the most famous figures in the history of Western art.

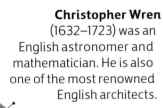

Christopher Wren (1632–1723) was an English astronomer and mathematician. He is also one of the most renowned English architects.

Top six

About 750 million people live in Europe. Here are the six most populated countries in Europe.

Russia
Around 143 million

Turkey
Around 81 million

Germany
Around 80 million

France
Around 67 million

Britain
Around 65 million

Italy
Around 62 million

Festivals of Europe

Europe celebrates some of the most exciting and unique festivals in the world.

La Tomatina, Spain

This huge tomato fight takes place in the small town of Buñol every year. Festivalgoers pelt each other with tomatoes for fun. The celebrations also include music, dancing, and parades.

Around 150,000 tomatoes are used every hour in this tomato fight.

Kettlewell Scarecrow Festival, Britain

For two weeks in August, this village comes to life with hundreds of whimsical straw-stuffed mannequins.

Busójárás, Hungary

Local men parade through the town wearing fearsome traditional carved masks to scare away winter during Busójárás. The festival goes on for an entire week!

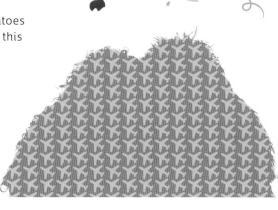

Water jousting, France

The city of Sète in France celebrates its patron saint with water-jousting tournaments throughout the summer. Jousters stand on boats and try to knock each other into the water!

True or False?

1. Busójárás is celebrated for a week.
2. Italy is the most populated country in Europe.
3. Water jousting is a winter festival.
4. Christopher Wren was a famous composer.

19

North America

North America

There are 23 countries on the continent of North America, and each one has its own unique culture, history, and landmarks. Here are just a small number of the places to see.

Famous sights

Fill in the stickers, and complete the names of these famous places in North America.

G _ _ n _
C _ _ y _ n

Hint: A huge crater with a river running through it.

C _ _ _ t _ l
_ _ i _ d _ n _

Hint: A place where people from the United States government work.

N _ _ g _ _ a
F _ _ _ s

Hint: A huge waterfall between the United States and Canada.

G _ l _ _ n
g _ t _
_ r i _ _ _

Hint: An incredible bridge suspended over water.

C _ _ c _ é _
l _ _ á

Hint: The ruins of an ancient Mayan city in Mexico.

B _ _ f _
N _ _ i _ n _ _
P _ _ k

Hint: An area of amazing natural beauty in Canada.

Bald eagle

Black bear

Chipmunk

Yosemite National Park

Yosemite National Park in California is one of the most incredible parks in the world. It's filled with breathtaking waterfalls, valleys, and forests. People visit to go hiking, fishing, and rock-climbing.

Mount Rushmore

Mount Rushmore in South Dakota is one of the most famous landmarks in the world. The portraits of four former American presidents are carved into the rock.

Draw your own portrait here.

The most popular tourist destination in North America is Times Square in New York City. Around 50 million people visit it every year.

Steller's jay

Bighorn sheep

Mountain lion

Bobcat

Mule deer

Coyote

Yosemite is home to many wildlife species. Add the stickers of the animals to the scene, and check them off.

Bald eagle ☐	Steller's jay ☐	Bighorn sheep ☐
Black bear ☐	Mule deer ☐	Mountain lion ☐
Chipmunk ☐	Coyote ☐	Bobcat ☐

More of North America

North America is the third-largest continent in the world. Of the 23 countries on this continent, 12 are islands in the Caribbean Sea.

Sand fairy

Next time you're at the beach, lie on your back in the sand. Then, wave your arms and legs up and down. When you get up, you'll be all sandy, but you'll leave a fairy shape in the sand! Decorate with pebbles, shells, and seaweed.

Most populated countries

North America is home to more than 580 million people. Read about some of the most populated countries on the continent.

United States

With around 330 million people, the United States of America is the most populated country in North America.

Mexico

Mexico has a population of around 127 million people. It is home to more than 30 UNESCO World Heritage Sites.

Canada

Canada is the second-largest country in the world after Russia. Around 36 million people live there.

Guatemala

Guatemala is home to around 16 million people. Even though Spanish is the official language, 21 Mayan languages are spoken in Guatemala.

Cuba

Cuba has a population of around 11 million people. It is home to more than 200 bays and 250 beaches.

Haiti

Haiti has around 10 million people. It is the most mountainous country in the Caribbean.

Beach love

North America is surrounded by oceans and has some of the world's best beaches.

Lion's Head Beach, Canada

Ideal for picnics, Lion's Head Beach also has camping areas, a marina, and a playground for children.

Birds of North America

North America is home to more than 760 bird species. Here are some common birds you might spot there.

The **peregrine falcon** can dive at 200 mph (321 kph). It is found across North America.

The **Baltimore oriole** is the official state bird of Maryland. Male orioles are known for their orange-gold feathers.

The **downy woodpecker** is a backyard bird, commonly spotted in Arizona and Queen Charlotte Island.

The **mallard** duck is found throughout North America. The male is known for its green head and yellow bill.

The **tricolored heron** is found in the coastal parts of North America. When hunting for fish, this heron makes quick turns like a ballet dancer.

Bowling Ball Beach, California

Bowling Ball Beach is known for the large, round rocks found there during low tide. This is a quiet beach where seals are sometimes spotted close to shore.

Cocoa Beach, Florida

Known for its consistent waves, Cocoa Beach is ideal for surfing. This golden sandy beach also offers activities like kayaking and dolphin watching.

Playa Ruinas, Mexico

Playa Ruinas beach has white sand and turquoise waters. There are well-preserved Mayan ruins that overlook the Caribbean Sea.

South America

South America

One of South America's most famous landmarks is Machu Picchu—an ancient hilltop city built by the Inca people. It was lost for hundreds of years, but it's now visited by millions of people every year.

Countries

The 12 countries of South America are Argentina, Bolivia, Brazil, Chile, Colombia, Ecuador, Guyana, Paraguay, Peru, Suriname, Uruguay, and Venezuela.

Backpacking

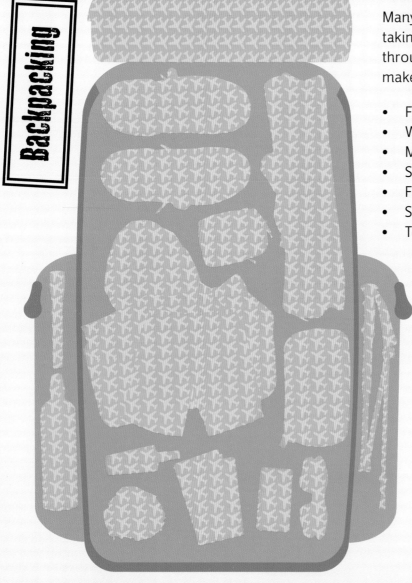

Add the sticker for each piece of equipment!

The Inca Trail

Many visitors travel to Machu Picchu by taking the Inca Trail—a four-day hike through the mountains. You'll need to make sure to pack everything you'll need!

- Food
- Water
- Map
- Sunscreen
- First-aid kit
- Sunglasses
- Tent
- Sleeping bag
- Sleeping mat
- Clothes
- Boots
- Phone
- Hiking gear
- Flashlight

Explore some more

There are 12 countries in South America, and every one of them is filled with incredible places to see and experience. Here are a few of the most well-known.

Welcome to Machu Picchu

There are lots of people exploring the amazing ruins. Can you find and circle these tourists?

- Someone taking a selfie
- Someone checking a map
- Someone in green shorts
- Someone sitting on a rock
- Someone feeding an alpaca
- Someone with a bottle

Add the correct sticker for each of the landmarks.

Amazon rain forest

Angel Falls

Brasília Cathedral

Easter Island

Christ the Redeemer

Salar de Uyuni

25

More of South America

South America is the fourth-largest continent in the world and has 12 countries. It is surrounded by the Caribbean Sea in the north, the Pacific Ocean in the west, and the Atlantic Ocean in the east.

South America's most populated countries

South America is home to around 426 million people. Here are some of the most populated countries.

Name: Colombia

Population: Around 49 million

Fun fact: Caño Cristales in Colombia is a series of rivers, waterfalls, and streams. It is known as "The Liquid Rainbow" due to its vivid colors.

Name: Brazil

Population: Around 200 million

Fun fact: Brazil is the largest producer of coffee in the world. The country has held this position for almost 150 years.

Name: Argentina

Population: Around 40 million

Fun fact: Ushuaia is a resort town in Argentina. It is the southernmost city in the entire world, famously called the "End of the World."

Fact finder

Every country has famous landmarks that attract tourists from all over the world.
Can you list five such popular places in your country?

4

Name: Peru

Population: Around 31 million

Fun fact: Peru is famous for its Inca history.
It is also home to the giant Andean condor,
the largest flying bird on Earth.

5

Name: Venezuela

Population: Around 29 million

Fun fact: Venezuela is one of the most
biodiverse countries in the world. It
has over 25,000 species of orchids.

6

Name: Ecuador

Population: Around 16 million

Fun fact: Mount Chimborazo
is an ice-capped volcano. It is
Ecuador's highest mountain.

 Keep reading to know more about South America!

Saying hello!

Over 300 languages are spoken in South America. The
three most spoken languages are jumbled below. Match
the colored speech bubbles with stickers. Then see if
you can guess which language each "hello" is written in.

usoeuPgter

_ _ _ _ _ _ _ _ _ _

sipahSn

_ _ _ _ _ _ _

niglhsE

_ _ _ _ _ _ _

Asia

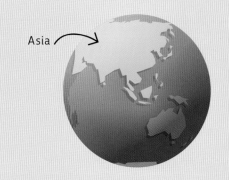

Asia

Asia is the world's largest continent and home to half of all the people on Earth. It's full of lots of amazing places to visit!

The Taj Mahal

The Taj Mahal is a beautiful palace in India. It was built by Shah Jahan in memory of his wife, Mumtaz Mahal, who is buried there.

The Taj Mahal is covered in precious stones.

Finish the other half of the Taj Mahal, and color it in.

Mount Fuji

Japan's tallest mountain, Mount Fuji is a volcano near the city of Tokyo. Mount Fuji is very important to Japanese culture. Use the stickers to complete the picture below.

More than 200,000 people climb Mount Fuji every year.

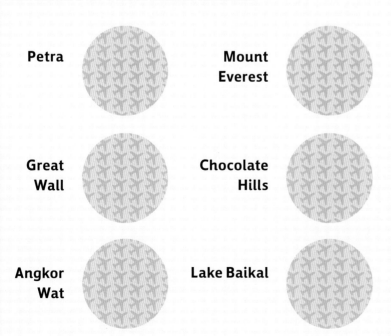

Other landmarks of Asia

Add stickers for these Asian landmarks.

Petra

Mount Everest

Great Wall

Chocolate Hills

Angkor Wat

Lake Baikal

L	H	O	X	O	E	V	A	S	P	Y	C	W	H
J	B	Y	V	B	F	K	N	V	E	C	H	J	O
W	J	F	H	W	D	J	G	S	T	E	O	M	A
B	U	P	E	T	R	A	K	P	Z	Z	C	O	N
H	L	G	D	L	Q	X	O	O	A	I	O	U	G
E	V	H	R	A	Y	G	R	I	W	X	L	N	K
F	K	M	V	N	O	R	W	D	J	T	A	T	O
J	O	F	K	Z	K	E	U	F	D	Q	T	E	R
J	L	A	K	E	B	A	I	K	A	L	E	V	W
Y	O	F	U	I	D	T	S	B	J	K	H	E	A
O	J	B	K	W	Z	W	F	A	W	B	I	R	T
B	P	R	Z	K	H	A	L	I	Y	A	L	E	H
Z	A	W	V	L	Z	L	H	L	Y	Z	L	S	Y
G	D	F	W	F	V	L	W	B	H	J	S	T	K

Next, try to find them written in this grid.

More of Asia

Asia is one of the most diverse continents. Around 2,300 languages are spoken across the continent by a population of over 4.3 billion people.

Asian food

Asia offers a wide variety of food. Every country on the continent uses different ingredients and spices to make the food flavorful!

Most populated

Here are the six most populated countries in Asia.

China
Around
1.3 billion

India
Around
1.3 billion

Indonesia
Around
263 million

Pakistan
Around
208 million

Bangladesh
Around
159 million

Japan
Around
126 million

Sushi and Sashimi, Japan
Sushi is vinegar-soaked rice served with or without raw fish. Sashimi is raw seafood like salmon or tuna, served without rice.

Butter chicken, India
Butter chicken is a popular curry dish made in a tomato gravy. It is usually served with flatbread.

Falafel, Israel
Falafel is a deep-fried ball made from ground chickpeas or fava beans. This yummy snack can be eaten alone, with salad, or with pita bread.

Natural wonders of Asia

Asia is the largest continent in the world and home to many stunning natural wonders. Match the color of the box with the frame to find the stickers.

Food journal

Next time you travel to a new place, keep a journal. List the dishes you would like to eat. Check them off the list when you've tried them.

Halong Bay, Vietnam

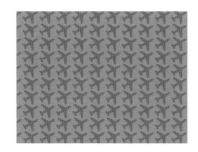

National Forest Park of Zhangjiajie, China

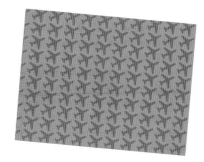

Okama, Japan

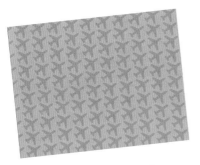

Kuang Si Falls, Laos

The Valley of the Geysers, Russia

Mount Bromo, Indonesia

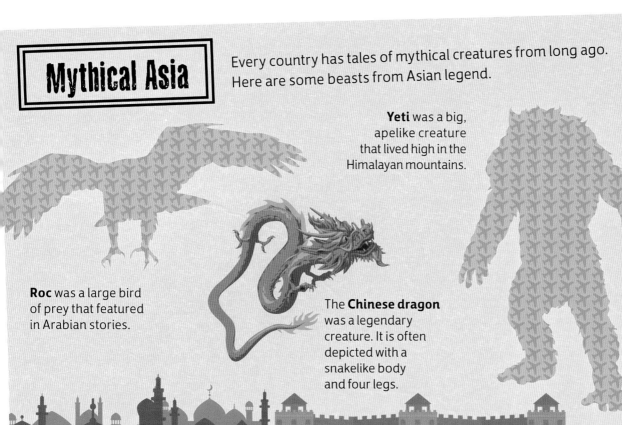

Mythical Asia

Every country has tales of mythical creatures from long ago. Here are some beasts from Asian legend.

Yeti was a big, apelike creature that lived high in the Himalayan mountains.

Roc was a large bird of prey that featured in Arabian stories.

The **Chinese dragon** was a legendary creature. It is often depicted with a snakelike body and four legs.

Africa

The continent of Africa has a massive 54 countries and is home to more than a billion people! Let's explore some of its most famous places.

Africa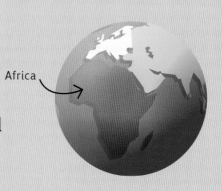

Sights of Africa

Unscramble the names of the places, and use the clues to find out where to place each sticker.

EHPDRTAISYM

Hint: Watch out for the mummies in these ancient Egyptian buildings!

ELRVRENII

Hint: Let's sail along the longest river in the world.

ICOVRTLIFAASL

Hint: Can you see the beautiful rainbows in this amazing waterfall?

NRMILOKTAIMAJ

Hint: This stunning landmark is Africa's tallest peak.

ASEHARDTASER

Hint: Make sure you drink lots of water before venturing into this hot place.

IERSTNEGE

Hint: Keep an eye out for all of the amazing wildlife!

MT. KILIMANJARO

VICTORIA FALLS

SAHARA DESERT

NILE RIVER

THE PYRAMIDS

SERENGETI

Kruger National Park

Many people travel to Africa to go on safari and see some of the incredible wildlife. One of the most famous safari grounds is Kruger National Park in South Africa.

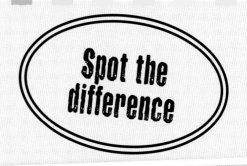

Spot the difference

There are eight differences in these two pictures.
See if you can spot them!

Not everyone can visit Kruger National Park to go on safari, so why not come up with a safari in your mind?

Take turns with a friend naming animals starting with each letter of the alphabet—ant, bat, cat. How far can you go?

Connect the dots

Draw a line through the dots to reveal an image.

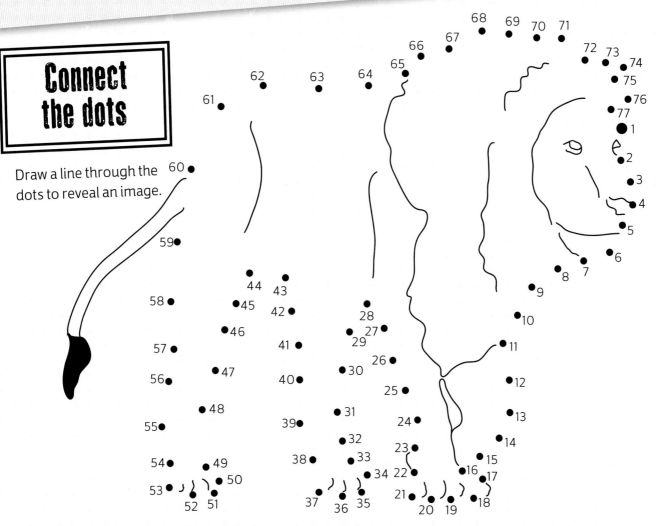

More of Africa

Africa is the second-largest continent. It is home to over a billion people. Let's take a look at some of the most populated countries in Africa.

TRAVEL DATA

Africa is surrounded by bodies of water on three sides.

The Nile in Africa is the longest river in the world.

Nigeria

Nigeria is the **most populated** country in Africa, with around 190 million people. It is also known as the "Giant of Africa."

Democratic Republic of Congo

The Democratic Republic of Congo is located close to the equator. It is the **fourth-most-populated** country with around 84 million people.

South Africa

South Africa has a population of around 57 million people and is the **fifth-largest** country by population. It is very rich in minerals.

Egypt

Known for its ancient monuments, Egypt is the **third-most-populated** country in Africa. It has around 98 million people.

Ethiopia

Located on the Horn of Africa, Ethiopia is the **second-most-populated** country. It has a population of around 100 million.

Tanzania

Tanzania has a population of around 56 million people. It is the **sixth-largest** country by population.

Africa's Great Migration

Africa's Great Migration is considered to be one of the most spectacular wildlife displays on Earth. More than two million wildebeests, gazelles, and zebras make a long journey across Tanzania and Kenya every year in search of better grazing areas.

African history

The stunning monuments and ruins of Africa tell us about its rich history. The continent has seen the rise and fall of several powerful empires.

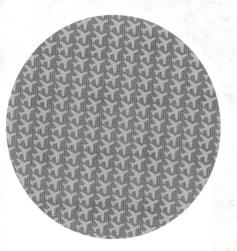

The Mali Empire
This empire was known for its enormous baked-mud buildings—they had to use mud because stone was not readily available.

The Kingdom of Kush
The area surrounding the capital of Kush is known for its 200 plus pyramid ruins—more than in all of Egypt.

Great Zimbabwe
Great Zimbabwe was a fortress city. No mortar was used to build the rock structures of the city!

Quiz

1. Which is the most populated country in Africa?
2. Which animals are part of Africa's Great Migration?
3. What was the Mali Empire known for?
4. Which country is located on the Horn of Africa?

Australia

Although Australia is a country, it's a continent too! The continent is made up of 14 countries, including the mainland, New Zealand, Tasmania, Papua New Guinea, Fiji, and thousands of other islands.

Australia

Beach count

Bondi Beach in Australia draws a lot of tourists. Add the sticker for each item, and count how many of each one you can find in the scene.

Camera

Backpack

Beach ball

Palm tree

Flip-flops

Sunglasses

Landmark match up

There are some amazing sights in the continent of Australia. Match the sticker to the landmark.

Split Apple Rock, New Zealand

Great Barrier Reef, Australia

Tsunami Rock, Tonga

Sky Tower, New Zealand

Sopoaga Waterfall, Samoa

Q&A

1. How many countries are in the continent of Australia?

2. Which natural landmark in Australia can be seen from space?

Where to stay?

There are lots of options for places to stay on a trip to Australia. Add the correct sticker for each option, then follow the vacation checklist to select the perfect place.

Cabin
- Quiet location
- Near a campsite

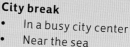

City break
- In a busy city center
- Near the sea

Camping trip
- In a campsite
- Quiet countryside
- Middle of nowhere

Sailing trip
- On the water
- Harbored in a noisy town

Beach hut
- On the water
- Quiet beach resort
- A short walk away from a harbor

Vacation checklist

- Quiet location
- Somewhere to go snorkeling
- Access to a harbor

Where to stay this time: ....

More of Australia

Australia is a huge island nation that lies between the Indian and Pacific Oceans. It is the smallest continent in the world. Australia is home to snowy mountains, deserts, and beaches.

Outdoor experiences

Most Australians live near the coastal areas, because it is cooler. Many Australians love the outdoors and enjoy a variety of different activities.

Australia is known for its **diving** spots. It has colorful coral reefs and purposely sunken ships that enhance the diving experience.

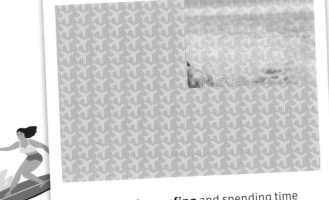

People enjoy **surfing** and spending time on sandy beaches. Australian beaches get some of the world's biggest waves.

Australian football, or "footy," is their local version of football. It has two teams of 18 players and is played professionally only in Australia.

The **Outback** is a vast desert in the middle of Australia. Even though it is hot and dry, there is a lot to see and do here.

Australia is home to many animals. Can you find out the names of 10 different animals that live there?

Find out

Australian wildlife

Australia has several unique animals that are native to the region.

Blue-winged kookaburras are large kingfishers. Their call sounds like a laugh.

Koalas love to eat eucalyptus leaves. They spend most of their time in these trees.

Emus are flightless birds over 5 ft (1.5 m) tall. They are the second-tallest living birds.

Kangaroos have powerful legs and can jump very high. Females keep the babies in a pouch on their bellies.

Frilled-neck lizards have colorful skin flaps around their heads. They unfurl them when threatened.

Quokkas are sometimes called the happiest animals in the world. A quokka is about the size of a house cat.

Vacation journal

You can plan a vacation to anywhere in the world. Jot down the places, food, and activities that you think you'll enjoy the most. You can decorate the page with stickers, too.

Time to start planning your trip!

The things I want to try during my vacation are _____

Draw a vacation destination here.

Page 4 Q&A: South Africa. **Page 6 Q&A:** Osaka. **Pages 8–9 Find and count:** Teddy bears (3), Airline staff (5), Security guards (3). **Page 10 Q&A:** Qamdo Bamda Airport, China. **Page 11 Can you?:** 1. College Park, Maryland, 2. Istanbul Airport, Turkey, 3. El Alto International Airport, Bolivia. **Page 13 Quiz:** 1. Passenger plane, 2. Yes, seaplanes, 3. Glider, 4. Supersonic plane. **Page 15 Where on Earth?:** Paris, New York, Cairo, Sydney, Rome, Shanghai. **Capital cities:** 1. Beijing, 2. Bangkok, 3. Buenos Aires, 4. Ottawa, 5. Athens, 6. Berlin, 7. Nairobi, 8. Abu Dhabi. **Page 16 Quickest line:** Line 2. **Page 17 Souvenir shopping:** You can buy the bag and mug and have €2 left. **Page 19 True or False?:** 1. True, 2. False, 3. False, 4. False. **Page 20 Famous sights:** Grand Canyon, Capitol Building, Niagara Falls, Golden Gate Bridge, Chichén Itzá, Banff National Park. **Page 27 Saying hello:** Portuguese, Spanish, English. **Page 28 True or False?:** 1. True, 2. True. **Page 32 Sights of Africa:** The Pyramids, Nile River, Victoria Falls, Mt. Kilimanjaro, Sahara Desert, Serengeti. **Page 35 Quiz:** 1. Nigeria, 2. Wildebeests, gazelles, and zebras, 3. Baked-mud buildings, 4. Ethiopia. **Page 36 Beach count:** Camera (4), Backpack (2), Beach ball (5), Palm tree (3), Flip-flops (2), Sunglasses (4). **Page 37 Where to stay?:** Beach hut. **Q&A:** 1. 14, 2. The Great Barrier Reef.

Page 8–9—Find and circle:

Page 14—Find your way:

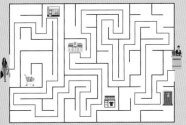

Page 29—Other landmarks of Asia:

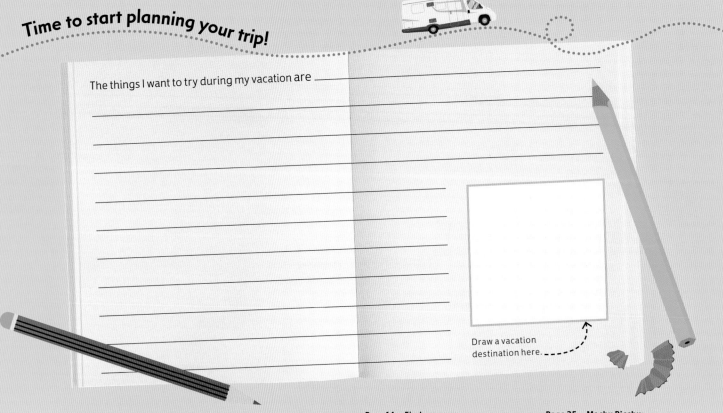

Page 25—Machu Picchu:

Page 33—Spot the difference:

Around the world

United States

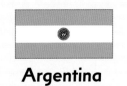
Argentina

Madagascar

Britain

Australia

Brazil

Russia

Finland

India

Japan

South Africa

China

Canada

What kind of vacation?

6-7 Popular travel sights

Petra

Northern lights

Great Sphinx of Giza

Colosseum

The Great Barrier Reef

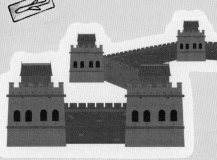

The Great Wall of China

The Statue of Liberty

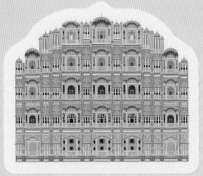

Hawa Mahal

Extra stickers

Greece

Norway

Ethiopia

Turkey

Germany

8-9 At the airport

Check-in checklist

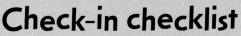

Put the remaining stickers anywhere you want.

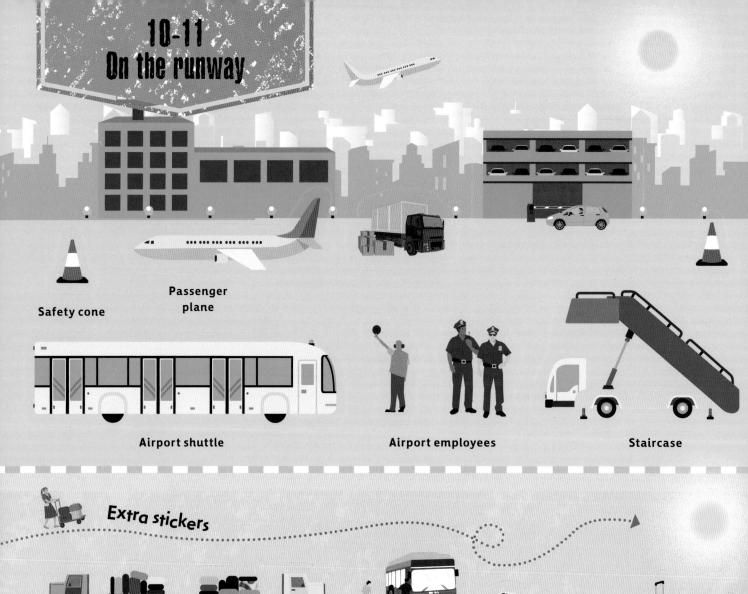

10-11
On the runway

Safety cone

Passenger plane

Airport shuttle

Airport employees

Staircase

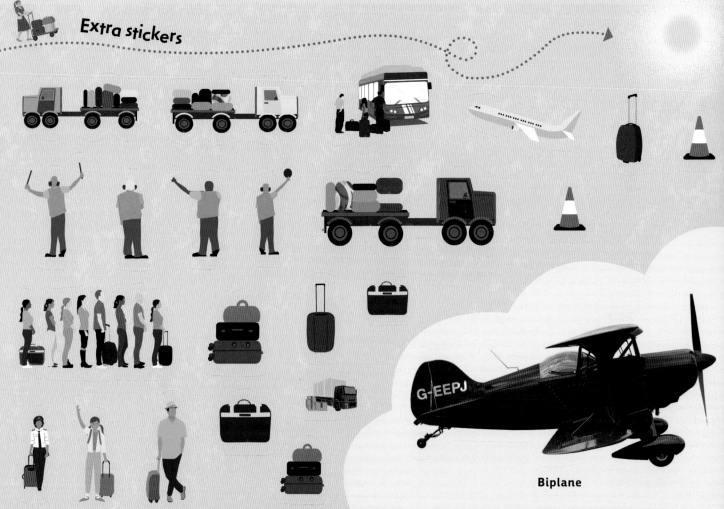

Extra stickers

Biplane

G-EEPJ

Put the remaining stickers anywhere you want.

Passenger plane

Balloon aircraft

Seaplane

Leisure aircraft

Jet plane

Supersonic plane

Extra stickers

Terrific towers

Leaning Tower of Pisa

Atomium

The Shard

La Sagrada Familia

Eiffel Tower

Extra stickers

Stonehenge   **Leaning Tower of Pisa**   **The Shard**   **Eiffel Tower**   **Trolltunga**

Giant's Causeway   **Matterhorn**   **La Sagrada Familia**   **Atomium**   **St. Basil's Cathedral**   **Colosseum**

European artists

Ludwig van Beethoven

Christopher Wren

Vincent van Gogh

Top six

Russia

Turkey

Germany

Britain

Italy

France

Festivals of Europe

Busójárás

La Tomatina

Kettlewell scarecrow

Water jousting

Extra stickers for fun

Travels around North America

Grand Canyon

Chichén Itzá

Capitol Building

Niagara Falls

Banff National Park

Golden Gate Bridge

Extra stickers for fun

Yosemite National Park

Steller's jay

Bald eagle

Coyote

Mountain lion

Bobcat

Chipmunk

Bighorn sheep

Mule deer

Black bear

Extra stickers for fun

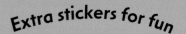

Birds of North America

Downy woodpecker

Baltimore oriole

Peregrine falcon

Mallard

Most populated countries

United States

Cuba

Mexico

Canada

Guatemala

Haiti

Beach love

Playa Ruinas, Mexico

Lion's Head Beach, Canada

Bowling Ball Beach, California

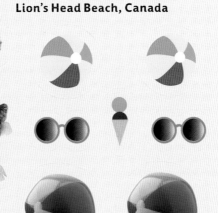

Put the remaining stickers anywhere you want.

Backpacking

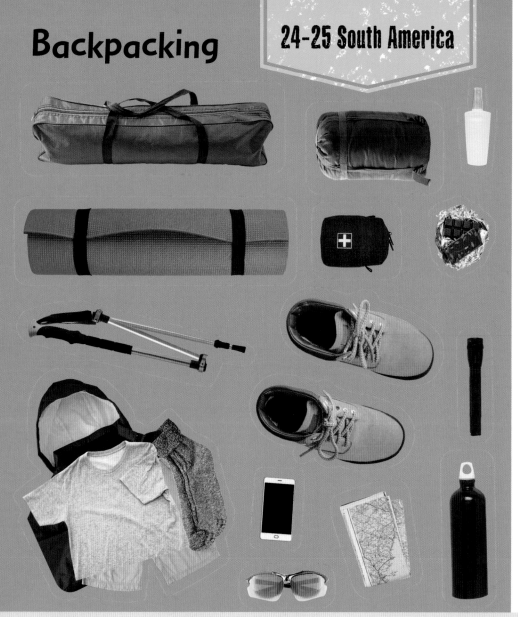

Explore some more

Brasília Cathedral

Salar de Uyuni

Easter Island

Angel Falls

Christ the Redeemer

Extra stickers

Amazon rain forest

South America's most populated countries

Ecuador   Peru

Venezuela   Brazil

Colombia   Argentina

Saying hello!

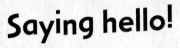 

Olá   Hola

Hello

Nǐ hǎo   Namaste

Vietnam   Morocco   Germany   Spain   Israel

Lebanon   Nigeria   Jamaica   Papua New Guinea   Peru

Italy   Pakistan   Portugal   Hungary   Thailand   New Zealand   Kazakhstan   France

Mexico   North Macedonia   Sweden   Greece   Norway   Ethiopia   Seychelles   Switzerland

Mount Fuji

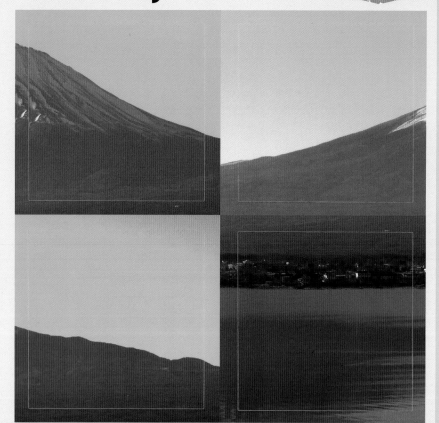

Other landmarks of Asia

Angkor Wat

Lake Baikal

Great Wall

Petra

Chocolate Hills

Mt. Everest

Extra stickers

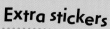

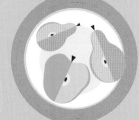

Natural wonders in Asia

Most populated

National Forest Park of Zhangjiajie

The Valley of the Geysers

Okama

Kuang Si Falls

Japan

China

Bangladesh

Indonesia

Pakistan

India

Asian food

Sushi and Sashimi

Falafel

Mythical Asia

Roc

Yeti

Put the remaining stickers anywhere you want.

Sights of Africa

The Pyramids

Nile River

Victoria Falls

Mt. Kilimanjaro

Sahara Desert

Serengeti

Extra stickers

Africa's Great Migration

Nigeria

Democratic Republic of Congo

South Africa

Tanzania

Ethiopia

Egypt

African history

The Mali Empire

The Kingdom of Kush

Landmark match up

Sky Tower

Great Barrier Reef

Sopoaga Waterfall

Split Apple Rock

Tsunami Rock

Where to stay?

Beach hut

Camping trip

Sailing trip

Cabin

City break

Beach count

Backpack

Camera

Sunglasses

Beach ball

Palm tree

Flip-flops

Extra stickers

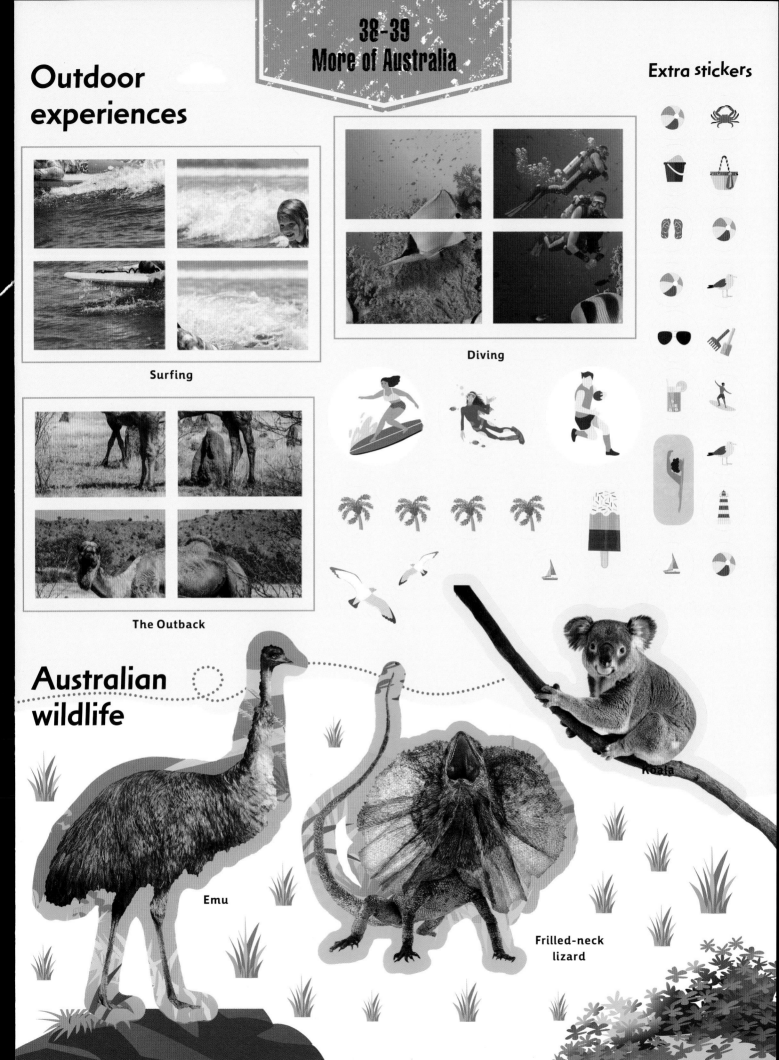

Outdoor experiences

Extra stickers

Surfing

Diving

The Outback

Australian wildlife

Emu

Frilled-neck lizard

Koala